DOWN SIDE UP

Healing Grief Through Poetry

DOWN SIDE UP

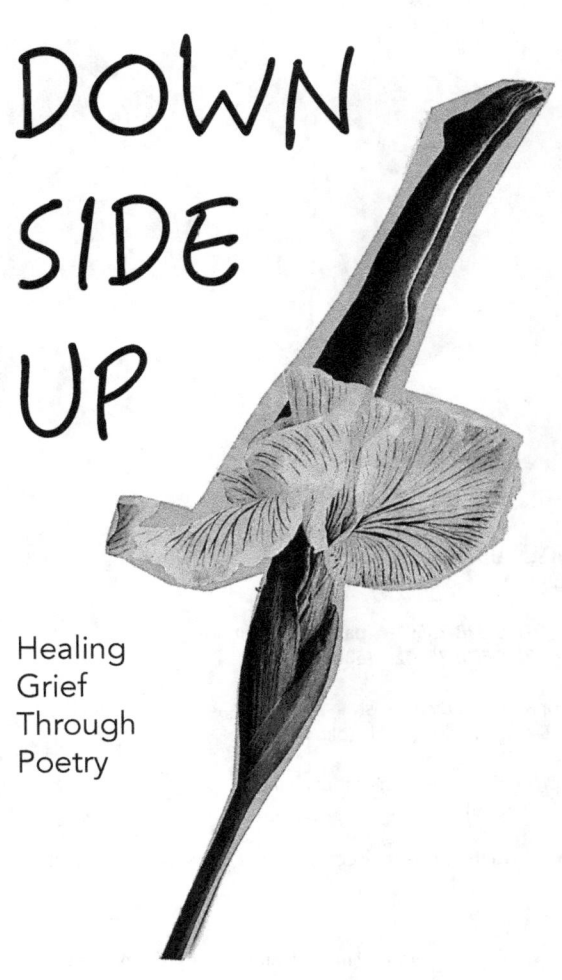

Healing
Grief
Through
Poetry

TRUDY A. BROSH

Down Side Up Is Copyright © 2020 by Trudy A. Brosh.
All rights reserved by the author.

ISBN: 978-0-578-75501-4 (paperback edition)
             978-0-578-75502-1 (eBook edition)

Interior art by Trudy A. Brosh
Cover Design: Redbrush, Lincoln, Nebraska

Sater & Sundal Publishing Company Inc.
Lincoln, Nebraska

To download the video to accompany this book, visit https://bit.ly/2YkoY1V

Printed in the United States of America by

Lincoln, Nebraska

For my children

For my daughter, Andrea, for all she suffered and the anguish she must have been in. May she be at rest and peace now. I truly believe that this solution was her total wish. She will suffer no more nor will I make her suffer more! I loved you so much Andrea!

I also want to give buckets full of thanks and appreciation to my loving son, Erick. He has been such a relief to me, as we have had many, many phone conversations, which have helped prop me up and guide me through. I love you so, so very much Erick!

For both of my children, I love you!

Here we are in happier times.

DOWN SIDE UP

Trudy Ann Brosh

In Remembrance

In memory of daughter

Andrea Brosh

April 14, 1972 - November 3, 1993

"Our Rose"

TABLE OF CONTENTS

PHASE I: SADNESS
Some of Andrea's thoughts in poetry before she died

PHASE II: MADNESS
Author's insights written in poetry after Andrea died

PHASE III: TO SUM IT UP!

PHASE IV: SUPPORTERS

PHASE V: A LULLABY
https://bit.ly/2YkoY1V

Notes

PHASE I: SADNESS

Poems of Andrea's

People

Big, tall
Short, small
God created them all
Why?
Life, death
Happy, sad
What for?
Joe, Harry
Sally, Sarah
Who???
Energy, power
Nuclear bombs
How come?
Questions, answers
Love, divorce
Pride, sorrow
Where to?
Peace, relief
Content, satisfied
When?

?Life?

September 26, 1991

Such Is Life!

Life is so strange. One day you are so full of energy and life. You're ready to go and take on the world from beginning to end, rough to easy, black to white, square to circle. Then you try to go to sleep and get rest to do all this! Tossing, turning, thinking. Dreams come and go, make sense and not. Wakenings bring new meanings new findings everything you felt the day before are gone and wiped out like a blackboard after the bell has rang! Sometimes leaving you with sour feelings, lemons, limes, rotten milk, sometimes blank like the tape you bought to record something yesterday. How is all of this put back together to make sense much less make you happy and vibrant again. Really makes a person wonder, wander, stray, look out at the world, go to sleep then wake up and try to make sense about it again on either a sunny day or even a rainy day.

Such is life!

September 26, 1991

Isn't it silly how emotions make a pen move? On boring days I try to sit down and write a poem I look back on other poems from the past and laugh! How stupid that I felt that way! And yet on my down days when my brain is working overtime (as usual) getting stressed and feeling blue I read over old poems and think wow! What a great piece of work this should be in a book! How do you figure? I guess it just proves then when you're up you are up and those downer poems don't make sense! But when you're down boy they sure hit the nail on the head! Then you hit days when you're in between and you write things like this. How strange!

"Longing for a Dream to Come True"

As I sit and try to think of a poem to write to you
Words pass through my head
Phrases from songs I hear on the radio
Over and over I hear them
And day after day I think of you
My tall dark and handsome
My knight in shining armor
The love of my life
My dream come true
But the one thing that's in the way
Is where are you
Who might you be
Holding on for the day that I meet you
Holding on for the good times that will come
The love that will be everlasting
The joy of being with you.
Till death do us part
Tiptoeing through the grass
During sensual and luscious times
Absorbing your every touch your every breath
Knowing you, wanting you
You wanting me caressing me
In no way I have ever been touched
Sharing our lives
Children at our legs
Feeling you inside of me
Please say you'll stay forever
Inside of me!

I will love you truly, faithfully and most preciously.
Forever and a day!

October 4, 1991

Confusion

Decision can be killers
They rule my every thought
What to do about the future
And then what not
I have some big decisions
That face me dead ahead
I don't know what to do
Sometimes I'd feel better dead
Why is life so difficult
And love a wondrous game
I only want to be happy
But I'm always just the same
Worrying about my life
It's such a drag to do
And maybe some day
This worrying will all be through
Then maybe I can settle down
And have a child or two
With the man I love for life
Or will we be through?!

                    To Terence because of Terence
                                   "1989"

Living life vulnerable and naïve
And stupidity rules my every thought or idea
Family I have let down and hurt
My mother whom I care most about in the world
She tries so hard but I can't get it through my ignorant wants
My father, which I don't know very well deep down
I use him for anything my greedy hands can get
When really all I want from him is attention and loving
And my brother very dear sweet guy,
Who is very close to heart but far from me
I treated him like a dope, and took from him, so he's backed away!
Friends and society are one very hard hurdle for me
People they come (as friends) stab me in the back then come back and stab some more
And I'm afraid to tell them straight up or start a fight!
And now a male figure, a true love, someone to love me, hold me
I've clung to so many guys thinking they were the ones
Giving myself to them and feeling a part of me being taken
Then when they were done I didn't feel what I thought I would
Love was far from where I lay and so hard to see
I felt nasty and unwanted once they left me and they'd used me
Revenge for those who hurt me only hurt me more
Because I turned around and used guys teasing and hurting them!
Just to prove 2 wrongs don't make a right they make it worse!

Then when I did find my first love and I couldn't handle the relationship
I couldn't get control over my feelings and his and combine them together
So when we parted and our love was through I found it hard to love again
I gave so much of myself to him that I even find it hard to love myself at times
And this is how I feel about it all
I have been hurt and have hurt
What has happened to me, I turned around and did to others!
But now that I've grown I've learned from those mistakes
I've learned to handle what I get better and to still treat them well
My family is a lot closer to me
Friendships are lasting longer and are a lot more fun now
But of course love is still a no go but I've learned to be patient and be picky!
I'm somewhat confused on some things in my life
But I'm gonna sit back and do my part and let the rest come!
The word us means so much to me
And the feeling of the need to be
I'd cling to many guys just wanting to be seen
For what I am and what's inside of me
Then giving myself to them in ways that were unreal
To my belief of how I should really feel
They took from me the parts that really hurt
Then shoved me away, kicked me to the curb
Feeling nasty and unwanted
My mind was now haunted
So taking to revenge in ways unmentionable

I really made myself into a fool.

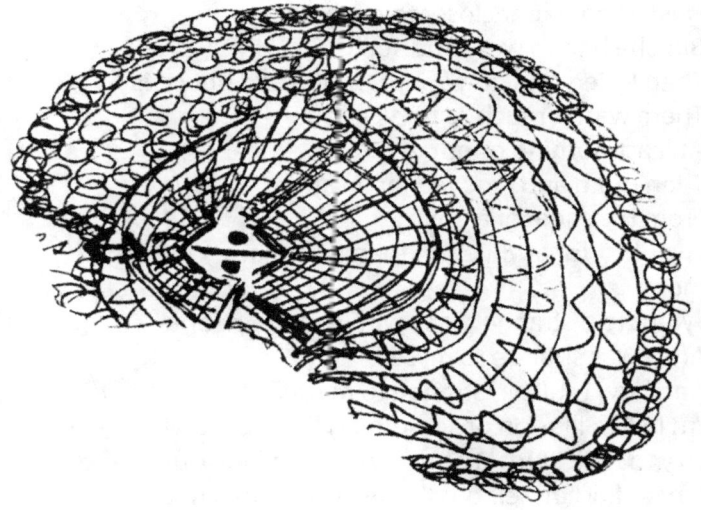

Changes

Changing every day
When I was at home
With my friends
I was immature and careless
Then I quit school and things changed
I tried to work but the hours
I could not handle
I tried to keep in touch with my friends
But they were too busy
I also tried to get closer to my mom
But she had to work and such
Then I tried thinking about my life and how it is
There wasn't much to think about
At least nothing good
Then mom and I moved far away
From that hole of a town
I was lost for a while but then I went away from my mom
I went to a strange place with strange people
And I was strange to myself
And now I still am strange to myself
I'm lost in illusion or something I don't know!
I try to look at reality but it seems to fade out on me
I try to find myself but I'm always in imagination land
Imagining how my life could be and ifs flying all around me
But the more I think about it the harder I'm trying to come to reality
Reality that I _am_ 16 and _in_ Job Corps
Reality that I have to be on my own after this place
Reality about myself whoever I am!

Someday I hope to find myself and show the world who I really am
But till then I will keep on changing but thanks to my mom and the people who have helped me form the guidelines and knowledge to lead me down the right road so that when I change it is for the better!

Blind

Am I blind to see what he really means to me
Is he just another guy to satisfy me
Satisfy me in many ways such as love sharing
Or is it just because he is there to hold
Just there to call my own so as to look good to others
I think it's love but how can I be sure
Is there a question to ask or a game to play
Or do I just sit back and take my time to find out
What has started here before me
Is it a relationship full of good things and love
Or is it a "thing" that happened out of desperation and need to be
I thought I was sure about this at once
Not in the beginning for that was too soon
But a couple months down the road
And now almost a year later
Also many problems, pains and heartaches
I've looked at us many times over
And I wonder what are we for truthfully
Are we acting out of desperation for some being
Or is it for growth of a relationship
I've not yet come to a conclusion
Am I seeing clearly as to what will happen
Or have I been blind to the happy thought of the word "us"

My Mom

My mom is the greatest human being I know
She is not only my mom who raised me from a baby
But she is a cheerful, warm, sensitive, loving, wonderful person
My mom and I didn't used to get along very well
We yelled and hollered and pushed each other around
But I hurt her not only physically but mentally too
And to this day and forever more I will regret it
I have grown to love her for so many things
And the one thing I most admire her for is staying by my side
After all I put her through and all I did
She still loves me and that means everything to me

Love

I'm told love is there somewhere
That someday I will have a true love
But it's hiding from me
Every time I turn the corner
There is another roadblock in the way
And each roadblock gets harder
And it hurts even more to look back
But what really hurts is to look forward
Because all I see anymore are roadblocks
I straddle them and they are gone
What seems to be my love disappears
Like ashes in the wind
And a piece of my heart goes with those ashes
At one time I had so much love to give
Now I'm afraid to love myself
Please Lord help me to see the light
I don't want a blinking light to straddle
I want a light that will burn forever
Before I've lost my heart and mind
Before my life is over and through
I will find my true love
And together we will be loving and true

Notes

Notes

PHASE II: MADNESS

Two years of Trudy's Mind in Poetry

INTRODUCTION:

I have been compelled to put the words on the pages of this book. It has taken buckets of tears, thousands of sleepless nights, many many days of cursing, swearing, hating, blaming, damning, self hate, hate of others and whatever the mind can think of doing to you; it has done it all! Always asking, "What if?" Trying to change what has happened!!

It has been over 25 years, and all those years seem to have been agonizing.

Have you figured it out?

SUICIDE

It was November 3, 1993, that the words that follow seemed to flow out of my head and onto the paper in rhyme. I am not or never have I aspired to be a poet. It started with the first time I was hospitalized and praying to die.

Soooooo

It goes.

Dear Ann

It's been a long day here at the hospital!

I still have not gotten on since loosing you. You were everything to me. I was so proud of you. You were doing so well. Why didn't you let me or someone help you? The girls at work were there for you.

Are you all right now?
Did it work for you?
Did you know it was so FINAL!

FINAL! FINAL! FINAL!
I JUST WANT TO SCREAM!
I wish I weren't so bull headed
How am I going to live when you're dead?

Loving you always,
Mom

Pysch Patient Becomes Poet on New Drug

Just two weeks ago on May 21, 1994, a psychiatric patient 45 years old started to write in rhyme. DD as she likes to be called, had not written poetry since 4th grade. DD had been hospitalized for severe chronic depression due to the suicide of her daughter November 3, 1993. After testing, her doctor found she had tracking and paranoid psychosis along with depression. The doctor started her on a fairly new drug, Risperdal, for the psychosis. This drug is especially for anxiety. It calms down the patient to think clearer.

DD has been writing on the average of 2 poems a day since the 13th. The words seem to flow from her brain, and she would write them down.

DD is excited about her newfound talent and says she hopes to have the poems published some day.

(My first poem in the hospital)

Peter, Peter had a patient,
But he couldn't treat her.
So he put her in a mental cell,
And there kept her very well!

I am like a mother cow
 Who has lost her calf and am going mad
Trying to find it – crashing down gates.
 Off by myself in the pen, wanting to
Bolt and run!!!!!

Wondering

Two weeks in the hospital and home again
My life dreams, hopes, and goals, I am trying to win.
The stay was long and it was tough,
It was my heart they were trying to buff.
For my heart is broken aching and torn
Oh how can one person be so forlorn?
Andrea Andrea couldn't you see
What you left behind and how I would be?
Now I'm home two weeks later
Sitting here, not a whole lot better.
This house and all the memories
Don't seem to put my mind at ease.
Your bedroom, the hallway, the door you slammed
All in my mind the horror is crammed.
Sloshing and churning wreaking havoc on my brain
I'd like to get it under reign.
The medicine they gave me helps a bit,
But all still here in my heart a pit.
Time is to be the healer of my plight.
Rest and work to help end the fight
Struggle on to cure the pain,
Each day some sense to gain.
I'm trying, I'm trying, that's all I can do,
Chiseling out meaning of what to do.
To stay, to move, to work, to marry,
In my mind the thoughts I carry.
Each day goes by, not going forward
Stuck in time or looking backward.
Oh when, when will I step off the treadmill?
Only that they say, must I will.
So I sit here two weeks later, still pondering.
Will I ever get better? I keep wondering.

Too Much!

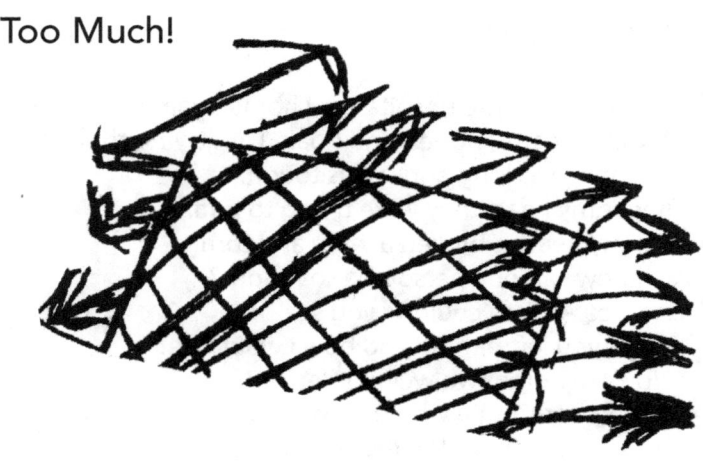

46-year-old and nothing to show,
Where I am going, I don't even know.
A home full of pretties, closet full of clothes
But my depression grows!
What will it take to get on track
To gain my life back?
Forgive and forget comes to mind
But in my heart, I can't find.
TOO MANY, TOO MUCH has happened,
My love is stiffold,
A way out I cannot find.
All the horrors my brain binds.
Trapped in a dangerous thinking mode,
To the devil I think I am sold.
Don't feel much better, don't feel much
Or I may get crunched!
Eaten alive by grief and fear
The end I feel is near.
How much longer can this go on
I want to run!!!!

January 24

A blank page now I sit and stare
My thoughts to write
My heart
To pour.
Inside of me there is a great big hole
A gap so big-
Ripped-
To the soul
I write and write to get all the pain out
It helps a bit for a while
But then somehow
It quits.
Oh to be that this tragedy had never been
I ache for the possibility,
Illusion,
Changed, it never can.
I've tried and tried so many ways,
Eluding the truth,
Escaping the pain for a bit.
But it comes back in front of me lays
Now I continue to write always in rhyme
Reality it shows up in verse now and then
But so far as this day
It is too sublime.

Fleeting Thoughts

I sit here now in this chair
No, I'm not anymore doing hair.
You see my daughter, my only girl
Died seven months ago in one big twirl.
She left without a word or a note
Nothing to ease my grief; nothing to quote.
I shout, I cry, I lay in despair
My heart, it seems never to repair.
I ask WHY all the time
Wonder and wonder.
What could possibly put this girl asunder?
If only, if only, I cry to the heavens
Her life to her that I could have given.
Now she is gone, her life to ever mourn
Sometimes, wishing I'd never been born.
Now, I am trying a bottled sedation—
Some kind of meaning to my life, an "equation"
Will it get better, or will it always be grim?
Someday, somehow on my face will I grin?
Oh heavens, oh heavens, will the pain ever lift?
That from you would be a great gift.
As I sit here in this chair, I think
My life too, could end in a blink

May 1994

I sit! and sit! and sit!
Oh so many cigarettes I've lit!
Waiting an watching
Searching and hoping
But all in vain
I'll never see her again.
The pain and agony
I can't get out of me.
What to do now?
And How?
Nothing matters, I seem not to care
The walls, I sit and stare.
A big part of me died that night
Now I've lost all sight
Of where I'm going, what to do
If only's I'm stuck — if only I knew!
Can't get a handle, can't get a grip
The pain in me, my heart rips
A new vision, a new purpose I must find
The answers I have not found
Days go by and nothing done.
I seem to want to run
From the world and hide my face
No more to do with the human race.
Most times I don't want to be here
But where then, I ask, <u>would cheer</u>?

January 25, 1995

Baby Girl

Baby, oh baby girl
You're life was such a whirl.
Smoking, drinking, gambling and sex
It was like you were under some kind of vex.
Running through life, not taking time to smell
Sometimes thinking life was hell.
The turn of two engines and off you went,
Where God only knows, have you been sent.
I feel so helpless, so hopeless, so lost
My baby is dead, my life's been crossed.
I know you are sorry, and I'm sorry too.
Oh baby, baby, what's mama to do?
Like a mother cow who has lost her calf,
I search and search on your behalf.
Seeking answers to questions I'll never know,
"They say" somehow out of all this, my life will grow!
So with a lump in my throat, and a hole in my heart
I'll travel down life's path, trying to find somehow, a way to restart
Baby, oh baby girl
You've gotten MY LIFE in such a whirl!

May 21, 1994

Hate

I still don't do well, beat myself up all the time! Life - a living hell. I can't go on this way much longer. I hate every day I'm on this Earth. Take me away from it all. I don't want to be here! I mean that. I'm burned. Everything I've chosen is wrong! I hate myself!

The Baby

I reflect on the day
That Ann's baby went away
It broke Ann's heart
And I didn't even know how much it did smart
Ann was quiet, kept the tears to herself
When she laid her child on the shelf.
Oh, she thought it all over, through and through,
Could she keep it? Oh what to do?
I filled her head with all reasons not
May my soul die and rot.
"What if?" I keep asking myself all the time
I hadn't been so critical and put all the blame
On her, my poor baby, so young and naïve.
Now here too, I have to grieve.
She left three weeks later
She somehow felt she must,
Now all I have left is dust.
Her baby she named Amanda Jo
Oh how I long to have both of them so.
What did I do?
Why did I think that?
I want my baby back!
Is this God's way to punish me?
So I hate myself, don't you see.
I did not try hard enough to understand,
Now all I want is to leave this land,
To be with Ann again
To be the way we've been!!

October 13, 1993

Dead Dead Dead

It is the day before thanksgiving 1994
I am alive but I don't know what for
Maybe it's just too soon to tell
Why I'm not dead and in hell!
My life has been like I've been in a daze
No purpose in circles like a craze
Day after day has gone by and now I'm 45
It seems I no longer now want to be alive!
What is the purpose? What is the use?
Just get out the rope and make the noose
Put it round my neck and off the rafters I'll jump
Fall dead on the floor with a great thump
All would be forever over
I'd be asleep in a field of clover
Who would miss me who would care
I sit and wonder on this chair
Nothing makes sense to me not even this poem
All I do anymore is lay and moan
I'm nuts I'm crazy I want it over
Oh to be dead in a field of clover.
Now my friend, you are gone forever.
My baby, my youngest, under a cover
Down under ground all alone and cold
Your soul to "life's love be sold"
Missing you is life's hardest toil
For months I cried, rolled up and coiled.
Wandering from job to job, searching and hoping
Trying to make sense of it, somehow coping
Now without my friend I must travel
To life's perils I alone must unravel
Somehow without you I must go
I'll always miss you my friend, I hope you know!

November 23, 1994

Missing My Daughter My "Best Friend"

The days are long and lonely
I sit and ponder only,
About the days that were bright and carefree,
When we lived together and laughed and shared to be.
We were best friends you and I
That's what I wanted, I thought I did try.
We shared life secrets and tribulations
Our life's triumphs to our elation.
We felt we could conquer all, together
Any trial or trouble we could weather.
We laughed — we cried, we chatted
On each other's backs we patted.
For all the wonderful tasks we two had achieved
We were strong — we would NOT be grieved.
But all that to an end it came
When you walked out, I'll never be the same!
I miss you, I love you, I want you back so
Oh why, oh why did you feel you had to go?
If I had only one wish
It would be that you'd be here, then we could hug and kiss!
Continue on as we had in the past
But see this is over, not possible, not defined to last
I think you were stubborn, foolish and selfish
But if this is what had to be, if this was your wish
Then as a friend, who am I to stand in your way?
I tried on that fatal night — I CARE I tried to say
I love you I understand
Let's talk I tried to demand.
Your mind, I think, was made up then
No more talking, laughing or joking
"I can't take anymore," your look conveyed
Why oh why did you have to have your way?

Out of the depths of darkness gloom and doom of pain
Is all of this grief in me selfish and vein?
Who am I to think that this is
Some kind of sick trick of HIS?
I just don't think I can take it anymore
My spirit is <u>broke</u> to the CORE!
Oh God are you there, yoo-hoo?
What, oh what, do you want me to do?
I'm stuck in one way thinking you know
Now I feel any day I'll walkout, I'll go!
Please give me an answer, give me a sign
For instance why do I talk in rhyme?
What, oh what, am I to do?
Give me an answer, please do!

Misery

Nothing oh nothing will bring Ann back
That in my mind does that fact lack.
Wishing — pleading — stomping or curse
Will not take away the fact we rented a hearse
She died! She died! She died!
To my mind seems like all have lied.
It can't be. It can't be. I cry and cry.
To change the outcome I try. I try.
Only in peril in pain and agony
My pleas not heard, it puts a drag on me.
Pulling me down more and more
I've reached the bottom only tears I pour.
Crying and crying seems only to show
The love that I felt would only to grow
Get greater and greater till I would burst
With pride to the world that my daughters first.
In my heart number one in all she would do
Because she was mine my life to ensue.
But that has been stolen from me
Her talents and gifts now never to be.
Oh what sadness. What pain, what agony.
I cannot bear the misery in me.
Nothing oh nothing will bring Ann back
Will my mind soon burst and crack!

My baby, my baby,
I want my baby!
How will I live now without her?
Nothing the same, for sure.
She is lost forever without a doubt
But my mind doesn't accept the thought
It hurts, it hurts, the pains so deep
Even the good memories are so hard to keep.
Everywhere I go, whatever I do
I always think in my mind of her so.
I don't even know if she wanted to go then
Who knew what on that night and when
I'm crying with self-condemnation and doubt
What my mind was thinking about?
Was it denial to me that she was that far gone?
What was going on, what had she done?
She wouldn't talk, she wouldn't listen
So at three I went to bed and then-
In the morning I found her in the garage-
I only hoped it was a mirage!!
I called 9-1-1 then, but oh so late
She had already met her maker's gate!
Why oh why did I not call someone sooner?
As my mother so insensitively said, "What a bummer!"
I sit now on that same stool as I sat that night
Wondering and wondering why I didn't put up more of a fight.
Why didn't I get her to talk to me?
To break down her door to see
What she was really doing in her room.
I thought she wanted space, I did assume
Oh she got her space oh that she did
Now she is forevermore dead!

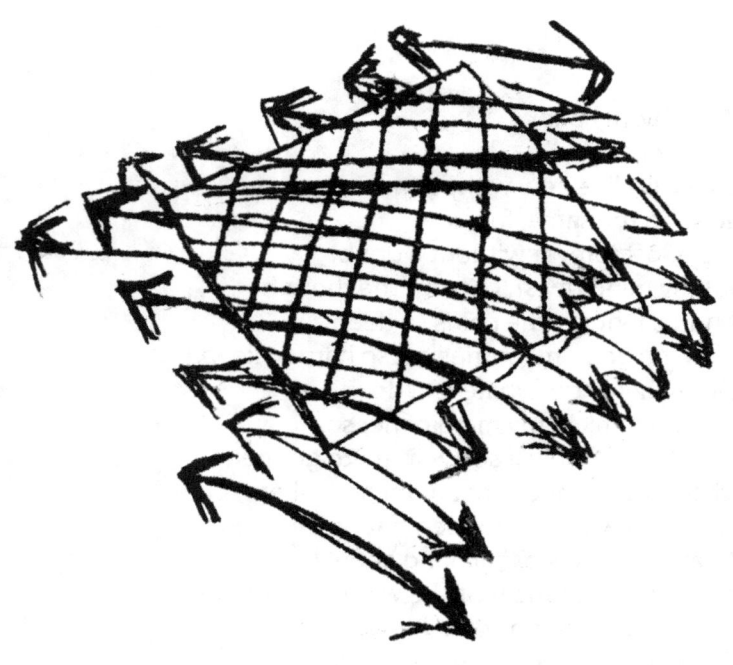

The more time that goes by
It seems the deeper I get,
Here on the bed I want to lie
My pillow all wet.
It's a damn shame I am here
To suffer this so
I want to leave this land I fear.
To get out, to go!

Life's Highway

It is very fast, curvy and broken
That long road that we all must journey.
Starting out is not too hard
For many signs are posted to show the way ahead.
Once we are on it and down aways
The turns and crossroads to us bays.
Should we pass, should we speed,
Shall I turn off here? A map we need.
Life's highway has no markers, no lines
We alone travel our way sometimes tangled like vines
To unravel the trip to make sense of it all
We ponder, we wonder, we try to keep on the ball.
Being alert stay on our side
So that we can try to have a smooth ride.
The curves are the worst to try and navigate
For they throw us down, to death we may gravitate.
But if we are to make the grade
Out of our mind these thoughts we must raid!
So we press our minds our eyes our ears
To life's perils, and calm our fears.
With keeping on life's broken road
The courage, faith, trust to self be sowed.
Yes we must keep true to our destiny
Or that road will "eat up the rest of me."

Reflections on Mt. Sequoah

I am home again
Here to sit all alone and spin.
The trip was only 3 days long
Not much time for prayer and song.
Classes, sermons, stories and such
To heal the spirit a whole bunch.
Yes it was a great healing time
Not too subtle not too sublime.
Got right to the core, right to the soul,
To fill the void, plug up that big hole.
Now here I sit alone and think
Will I make it or will I sink?
Oh, I can't go much further down
Yes then I will certainly drown.
Can I make it to the other side
The storms, the waves, will I ride?
If I had only chosen a sturdier boat
Instead of thinking that alone I could float.
I have been offered to come aboard
The Methodist steamship along with the Lord.
Praise God and all his miracles,
Now maybe my life won't go in so many circles
I'll jump on and try the ride offered me.
It makes sense don't you see
God sent the ship to carry his people forth
Safely surely for all He's worth
Yes we have to fan the flames
But we will do that in God's name
Here I sit at home again
Praying, seeking, my life to win!

"Fly High"

That crow was perched on the fence in the cemetery
I thought at first her presence was elementary.
But she danced on the fence with great agitation
As if she must have my full attention.
Then the thought came to mind
That it was I she was trying to find.
You see my daughter had been buried there
And I think the crow with me had something to share.
The crow watched and watched as she pranced and bound
To see if I glanced or turned around.
Then just as I turned to admire her cheering,
She seemed to wink, flew up and soared out onto a clearing.
What was she saying to me on that sunlit day?
The thought was immediate, it did not delay.
The crow had news I'd been looking hard for,
My daughter's flown on from her life that hurt so
And now when I see a crow flying free
I smile to myself and feel "peace in me."

> This was written when I got home from the cemetery. I made many trips the first year and brought flowers, flowers and more flowers!
>
> June 1994

"Settle Me Oh God"

Oh God I pray
That you guide me today
To get through yet another
Somehow better one after the other
Guide me — hold me — carry me through
That is what I pray for you to do.
I know you are present all encompassing
Your presence felt your healing rings
In my ears, my heart, my soul –
At each blood vessel you pull -
Settle me oh Holy one divine
So my life be given back smooth and fine.
Each day I need to know
That you are present you want me to grow
O God I pray
That you guide me today!

June 13, 1994

I want it all to go
Fast like a rocket
To help get rid of every facet
Of the pain and grief I bear now
Will it, pray it, stand it, HOW?

June 10, 1994

Peace

Peacefulness is what we achieve
When we let go and stop the mind to grieve.
For hanging on to all that bad stuff
Will only make our lives tough!
A smoother, less bumpy road we will take,
When we let go for our sanity's sake.
So stand up tall, stand up strong
Throw away all that have wronged
A better and richer life to lead
In my heart, plant a new seed.
Let go, let go, let go of it all now
For I have outlined in this poem, so you know why and how!

June 10, 1994

Cure of Hospital — Second Time!

To the hospital I must go
To help myself, to help to grow.
What I learn, what I take home
I only pray that the light, I see some!
To get over what the hell ails me
I must try to get better don't you see.
Get better so that I can erase
All of the pain that in me now I face,
It's not easy, it's not luck
That out of the murk I get myself unstuck.
Grasp onto all the information
Then with these tools and some imagination
Travel down life's path again.
Happiness and fulfillment trying to win
Time too, will help the hurt go away
That is what everyone, they all say.
How much? Only in ourselves to us be shown
The amount and length of it to show we have grown.
Out of the grief — the hopeless — the despair
Our own minds and hearts we leave to repair
So the hospital it stands for
Our lives to us be given back so we are better than before!

June 19, 1994

Let Go

Way deep down inside of ourselves
There is a longing to hang on, put the bad stuff on shelves,
In the brain we tend to hold
All of the tragedy to us be sold.
We hang on and on to all of the garbage
Till it eats out the insides I would wage
Now we have come to a day
When we must get all this stuff out of the way!
Erase it, unload it, pencil it out.
Out of the mind, through our mouths shout
Let it flow out to some place far
Out of our hearts and mind we must bar!

June 9

What is Love?

Love is an "I don't know"
Could it be that it is present to help us grow.
To understand in our hearts and try to weave
A pattern in us not to grieve.
For if love is present, then we have to feel
That all we care about is very real.
We care for family, friends, spouses and such,
And it seems sometimes that they don't give back much
But it is ourselves we tend to fool
For love binds us together, it is a great tool.
We must cultivate it, nurture to grow
So that our lives are better and we will sow.
To all we must show our gratitude
With a forgiving and loving attitude
Then we too will be actualized
And our lives be fortified
With love to guide and love to bear
We surely will get through all this, I swear!

June 9

Happy

Out of the darkness, the shame, the horror
Can I manage again to get out of the door
Pull myself out of the gloom and doom
Make my life brighter, happiness to consume
Will it get better? Will it real soon?
The life that I'm living or is it all too construne
Bring it around, bring it back full coarse
Scream to the heavens until I get hoarse
I want to be happy want to be all fulfilled
But can it happen, my heart longing be willed
Work hard, climb up that big hill!
To make the eyes sparkle again, it's a big bill.
Only with courage and hope I go on
The fight to be happy again will be won.
It won't always be smooth, won't be easy
The ride I take sometimes it will make me dizzy
If I work hard for this goal to strive
Then someday soon, my life it will thrive
Be happy, be happy, it's what I want back
If someday soon it happens then I won't totally crack!

June 5, 1994

Advice

Advice comes in several forms
Not always thinking, not always the norm
But there is too
A lot that can be headed, a lot to ensue.
Forge ahead, don't look behind
Seems to be the best taken in kind.
Will it be easy, will it be hard
Will the mind get burned and charred?
Not if you try to listen too
What could be the BEST in your heart to do!

June 1, 1994

Time Passages
Rock to the Clock

I sit and watch the clock
My body I make it rock
Rock back and forth in my chair you see
Wanting and waiting time to go, so soon my mind can be,
Clearer, open, lost of all grief
I'd like to make this misery brief!
How long will all this grieving take?
I hope not forever for sanity's sake.
Time seems to go ever so slow
When you are waiting for the mind to grow.
Yes grow out of all the misery and grief
With each passing hour they say there's relief.
The burden it seems to get easier to bear
So one quits to have such a blank stare.
Time now it seems there is too much
For healing, mending, grieving and such.
Soon the time it turns into months and years
And so our minds over different thoughts it veers.
Slowly slowly the clock will prevail
And our mind be mended, somehow unknown, it shall
Somehow unnoticed the progress made
But somehow the stumbling blocks are mislaid.
Out of the way so we may travel on
The new wave lengths we have been put upon.
With time passage life gets easier
It sneaks up, catches us, gets breezier.
Uplifts our spirits so we can soar
Gets to the heart, the spirit, the core.
Time then you see
Can be good to thee!

June 13, 1994

A Child's Gift to Parents!

Two people brought me into this world,
All pink and rosy, my toes and fingers curled.
They took me into their bosom solely
A gift from God they knew knowingly.
They nurtured, they mothered, they fathered so tender,
To strive for a good life so they could send her.
Many years have passed through the realm now,
It went so fast, they didn't know how.
But they were always there, all by my side
Taking life's ups and downs, somehow it seems in stride
They seem to be all knowing somehow,
To minimize pain and suffering so.
What knowledge and patience they seem to bear
Out of all life's perils, they were always to care.
Now it seems all clear to me
How wonderful and kind they have come to be.
Oh, it is true they have always been
But sometimes I'd wonder, I have not always seen.
My eyes are open now,
I know not how it happened, I don't know how.
Thanking them for who they are,
Will go on forever, down the road far!
A child seems to not always appreciate
What parent's sacrifice, to what lengths they gravitate
To protect — guide and nurture so
To what lengths in life they take to help a child to grow!
Now all I can do is say, "thanks Mom and Dad"
For all you have done for me, to make my life grand!!
To show you how much I love you so
I'll keep living the best life you've taught me to know.

December 22,1994

Climb Up

Sometimes I say to life go away
To be dead sometimes I sway
This suffering then would be over
I'd be left down under a cover,
Would not have to do a thing
No more worries no more life's sting!
But then I would never know
How my son, he would grow!
Into a husband? A father?
I would never know if he could weather
All of life's perils and tragedies
I would not be there to help put his mind at ease.
So what am I saying that would be best
Give all this rotten thinking away, give it a rest.
Live on, live long, don't you see
So together we can all climb that big tree!

Swallow It

The pills they go down so swell
Will they change me, can they make me well?
I take them at hours pre subscribed
Sometimes me thinks my minds been bribed.
The brain has been taken to somewhere far
The mind sometimes it seems to soar.
Above the old self and making a new one
Somehow to make me better to have some fun.
What happens when
I have to be without the pills, to be without again?
Will I really change to be better again
To my self my will, I will win.
How long do I take this stuff,
So as to make my life not so rough?
Weeks, months, years I fear
Somehow to get my mind in gear.
These pills they seem to go down so well
Are they real or do they just make the head swell.

Taking Romance

Now I'm thinking a new love would be
What a nurse suggested to me.
How to go about, when to start?
That is the question, how to play the part?
Not to force it, not to wish,
Get out and try it, find that big fish.
I know it takes patience, takes guts and all that,
But alone have so many years I have sat!
So with my new freedom and knowledge to bear
I must take the courage I must take a care
Yes, it is scary and chances are too,
That good men to find are too few.
But if I want my world fulfilled
I must take steps, to my life's be willed.
How to start, when to go, will I continue
I sit and wonder?
Keep dreaming and praying that some day soon
Your wish it be granted under the moon
Now I am thinking a new love would be
Just how it all happens remains to be seen.

May 25, 1994

AND the Grief Goes On

Ann, Oh Ann, where did you go?
Are you at the mall, maybe the zoo?
I've looked at the restaurant and the bar,
I've tried to look most anyplace you've been so far.
I can't find you anywhere, and you're not coming home,
You don't sleep here anymore and you don't phone.
It seems you have vanished without a note,
You forgot your cosmetics, you didn't even take a coat!
I'm going nuts without you here,
The worst goes through my mind, I fear.
Why won't you call or write a letter,
To tell me you're okay, so I can feel better.
I don't sleep very well, I don't want to eat,
I sit in the house, on that same seat.
On the chair I was sitting, where I saw you last,
Waiting for you to appear, oh so much time has passed.
It's been over a year now, that I have seen you.
When are you coming back? What did you plan to do?
I don't want to give up on you, coming back ever,
Reality is, it won't happen. NEVER! NEVER!

December 8, 1994

It's my birthday today
I should say a hooray.
I'm still alive but not living
Keep to myself not very giving.
I'm 46 years old today
Didn't think I'd make it, I must say!
Oh so many perils that I've lived through
Now at wits end, don't know what to do
Survived loosing the love of my life
I was sure I would marry him to forever be his wife.
Then there was the November marriage to Joe
It ended 7 years later, who was to know?
Tried several businesses the last one I lost it
Threw in the towel not another to own I'd quit.
My son at eighteen went to live with his dad.
It was a mutual decision, but oh it made me sad.
My daughter went to Job Corps just a year later
My sorrow and loneliness grew greater and greater.
She came back 2 years later, better and stronger,
But she died three years after I desperately miss her.
Lost my job of 3 years over owner insensitivity,
By now I'd lost all levity.
They'd carried me off to the loony bin by now
I got out 2 weeks later I'm not sure how.
I do work again now but it goes like a yo-yo,
The frame of mind I'll be in I never know.
Some days the grief of it all overbears me
Don't know who I am or where I want to be
So today I'm 46
I sit here and my wounds I lick

                                      December 12, 1994
                                          My Birthday

It is 5 days before Christmas and I still sit on this chair.
Sometimes all I do is sit and stare.
Think and think of what I could have done that fatal night
To stop Andrea from leaving, to make it all right!
I didn't call, I didn't try hard enough to calm her,
I'm guessing all of her grief caught up to her and consumed her
Now it's been 1 year 2 months later
I'm consumed with guilt it grows greater and greater!
Keep myself busy is what they all say to do
It helps now and then but the pain it still won't go
Now I face this Christmas without her
In my heart and mind all the memories stir
It hurts so to think of memories good or bad
They just seem to make me sad.
I pray she is with her maker now
At peace somehow.
When will I get to the point that I will
Accept what happened and my heart be still?
I know I never, never will fully understand it all
To Andrea now I call and call.
Yell sometimes at the top of my voice
Why, oh why? Was that your choice?
Andrea, I miss you so desperately
I don't feel it was a fair choice you see.
If you thought for a moment no one would miss you
You were totally off base, of course we all do!
You had fought so hard, done so very very well
I was so proud of you, everyone I would tell!
Now it's almost Christmas again
Oh I wish none of this had to begin.
To change what happened is all I think and wish for
But that present won't be granted ever, I hurt to the core!

December 21, 1994

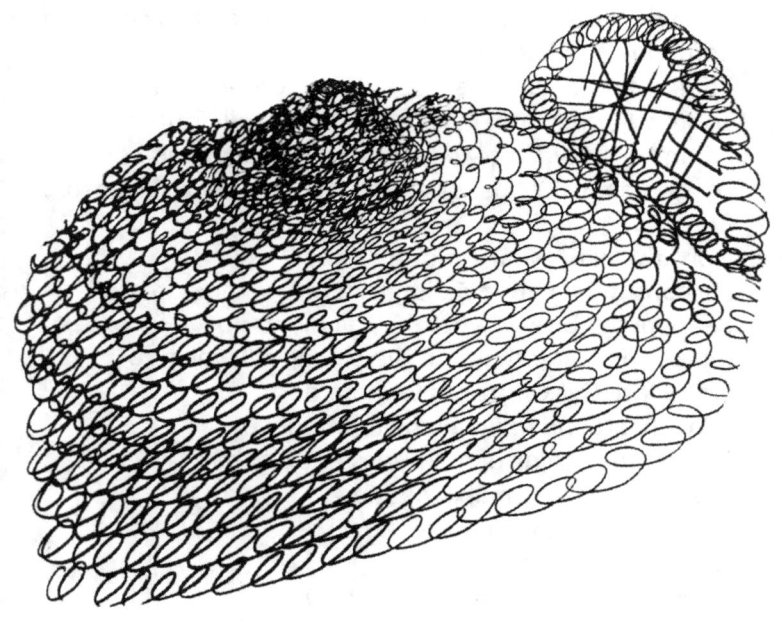

All I want for Christmas is my baby back
My baby back, my baby back and that's a fact.
All I want for Christmas is my baby back!

December 22, 1994

I sit alone in that same house, on the same chair
Thinking and thinking into a blank stare.
What should I do with my life now?
Where to start, move, go back to school, how?
All I do is get out to work
Come straight home after, social life I shirk.
How long will this bazaar pattern go on for
Surely, soon it must change so my life won't bore so.
Somehow I've become somewhat hermitized
Get out of the rut for a better life lies.
Go to a dance, dinner, or show
Join an organization, enroll in a class just get up and go!
No, no, no, my brain tells me
It's all in vain, a waste, just let me be
Like some kind of hold is weighing me down
Stagnated in life, I feel I'll drown!
I can only muster enough strength to go to work
Then straight home, TV, to bed with a book.
I feel my energy is all spent.
To do any more than just work I can't!
I feel I want to do more than just work
How to get out of the rut and find some kind of perk!
I sit alone in that same house, on that same chair,
Thinking and thinking into a blank stare.

December 22, 1994

Reflections Reflections

Reflect on life is all I do now
To get on with life how?
Why did I do what I did in the past?
The grief I feel about seems to last
I was living life without a thought
For those I care for, emptiness it seems I brought
Off to this meeting or to work I ran
It seems my children I did ban.
All of it seemed so ordinary to me
I felt I needed a life to be.
Did I overextend and limit my attention to them?
Is all I gave them gloom and doom?
This thought keeps running through my head
Now without my children it seems I'm dead!
One child left at twenty-one
She didn't think life was any fun.
She walked out one November night
Not to stay alive and put up any more fight.
Was she crazy or was it me?
I did not feel I abandoned her you see.
The other child I sent to his dad at eighteen
Hoping they could set a bond between
The colleges were closer I'd hope he would choose one
But soon then, the Army my son began.
Now he is further away in a far far state
Making his own way and college he does anticipate
He says now he is planning at Army's end
To come back and live with me, college to attend.
Oh I love/loved my two children so
Somehow it seemed to me I did <u>something</u> to help them grow.
I did what I did in the past and it is over
I just will have to live with the effect FOREVER!!!

Peace

Oh let it be peace in me
Peace of mind for me to see
Peace of soul and mend me now
Time to heal somehow.
Peace of heart to mend the broken
With the burdens carried unspoken.
Peace. Peace. Peace is what I pray for
To get me better so I won't be so
Bended down with misery
For the whole world to see.
I must get strong, that I will
Oh my heart be still.
For to move ahead I must
That too I will I trust.
Understand it, I never will
But yet I want to still
My sting is how I see it all
But the answer it is stalled.
Some day maybe it will unfold
The truth somehow told
Even then with answers known
The tragedy will still have been done.
Getting answers knowing more
Now I think what is the purpose for.
It happened, it's over, it cannot be redone!
But my secret wish is to change the outcome!

Happier New Year
Good Tidings Great Cheer!
Oh to think that a new years begun
Lord have mercy on all people's under the sun!

January 1, 1995

I had bought 2 brothers,
White blue point Himalayan cats
Basically a present to Andrea
I decided to sell them and I wrote:

Two little kittens went down the road
They don't know, but they've been sold.
Off to a new house where they'll be loved
Not in a laundry room will they be shoved
Fritz and Georgie are there names,
Blue point Himalayans marked the same.

How to fix a broken heart?
Are there prescriptions?
Exercises?
An arrow to point out a way to even start.
I hear that time seems to heal all wounds,
For each person the amount is different,
To try to wait out the clock
It's a lot harder than it sounds.
Patience is a good virtue to have
Without it we fight the wait
Want the pain over with
Wonder if we can live.
Prayer is recommended by the clergy
But in time of tragedy
It seems we doubt if there is a God.
And answers don't come with enough urgency.
Go back to work get the most votes
It gets your mind off your problems
Gets you out of the house,
But when you get back home that same feeling bites.
A therapist can be hired to talk it all out
But too few
Are trained
To really know what a broken heart is all about!
Keep busy is advice I hear every day
To keep the mind occupied
In essence it's a game with the mind
A race with the devil I must say.
When all else fails take a pill
Elevate the thinking
Slur the memory
When your own mind can't will

Empty — empty — empty — empty —
My heart, my head, my soul,
What in the world will it take
To make me whole?
They say you can move a mountain
If you only try.
This girl can't find the bulldozer
All I do is cry!
My heart is broken, split apart
My spirit downtrod,
All energy and will seem gone,
Nothing to applaud
The grief in me is overbearing,
It rips me right in two,
Can't seem to find the switch,
That reads "CAN DO!"

Clown Stitch

The crossed stitched clown was never finished.
She could not sit long enough
Her patience and attention were spent.
All she could do was to get it out and look impish!
She had smoking and gambling and men to date.
Oh heavens, she couldn't be late!
She ran off to school, to work or the bar.
Running in circles, running down roads
Where is she going so fast and free
Maybe now she's gone the gambit too far!
The last night I saw her with scissor and thread
She felt that life's perils were too much to dread.
Where, oh where, were you planning to go?
Did you think of those behind who
Love you and need you and want you to live!
The stitched clown you will not sew.

Stagnation

Now it's one day at a time, recovery is slow.
The medicine, I'm getting used to, breaking some
Tapes with my new tools.
Set some goals I must do
To give to my life something new.
A job — a move — save money for a vacation.
If not something I'll gravitate to stagnation.
So on and on I must truck
Down roads paths hoping to get unstuck.
Out of the cracks, the mud, the gravel,
My life's meaning must I unravel.
It is not easy, this road she,
For life's path can turn into an enemy
Not against others but our own selves.
Give grief to the brain cells.
Till sometimes our head it rings with bells.
Not for when it tolls, but clanging and clacking
A sense of direction we begin seeking.
So get back on the track, get back on the straight
It is what we have to do, it's only right.
The straight and narrow is a good rule
So that to aim, for me would be a good clue.
One day, one week, one month to set
So some perspective I will get.
Practical, sensible, whimsical, real
The goals I set to my heart I will feel,
If they are good or if they are bad,
To thine own self be true to make myself be glad,
Onward and upward with life's goals I say
How it will all come out, I pray?

Oh Let It Be Peace In Me

Oh let it be peace in me,
Peace of mind for me to see.
Peace of soul now and mend me.
Time to heal somehow.
Peace of heart to mend the broken
With the burden carried unbroken
Peace, peace, peace is what I pray for
To get me better so I won't be so
Bended down with misery
For the whole world to see!
I must get strong, that I will
Oh my heart, be still.
For to move ahead I must
That too, I will I trust
Understand it, I never will
But I want to, still!
My story is how I see it all
But the answer, it is stalled.
Some day, maybe it will unfold,
The truth somehow told.
Even then, with answers known
The tragedy will still have been done.
Getting answers, knowing more
Now, I think what is the purpose for?
It happened, it's over, it cannot be redone!
But, my secret wish is to "change the outcome!"

January 1994

Three months, 90 days
Since my Ann went away.
Sometimes it feels like yesterday
The pain started, like it was the first we parted.
I miss her so much every day,
There are so many many things I wanted to say
I love you from the bottom of my heart
One line to start
It's ok, don't worry, we will make it through.
Will sit down and figure out what to do!
We've made it this far you and I,
I don't want you to die!
If only, if only, if only in my mind I think
Reality sets in and my heart sinks.
She really is gone, forever!
To kiss her, embrace her again, never.
Oh so young and full of energy
How? I ask could this tragedy ever be?
I'll never know till my dying day
Why, oh why, my beautiful Ann went away.

January 23, 1994

Also

My heart is broke
My will is gone
What to do?
Now nothing gets done.
It seems I'm on a one-way street,
Going down hill,
Staring in space,
Showing all signs of defeat.
Can't get a handle,
Can't get a grip.
My bootstraps are broken
This thing I can't straddle.
I've looked at the option every which way
It seems most doors end up closed,
Or there is no energy.
Right here in this house and job I must stay!
I'm lonely, I'm lonely, I scream to all hear
But no one can fix it
I must alone.
I fear
I'm not well, don't feel good, am sick!
These pills
I am afraid
My heart they won't fix.

Angel Kisses

This Angel comes to you today,
She has many things to do and say.
She is here to give you strength,
She will go to any length.
She knows, she feels, she cares.
She is here to be aware.
Aware of all the emotion and all the pain,
Here to show you nothing will ever be the same.
She tells you she loves you and will always be near!
Prayers may help you to ease the pain and help to persevere.
This angel from heaven will help guide you through the grief.
Hold your hand, give you a kiss, help you try to understand,
That sometimes life comes like a thief.
She will find you at the bottom of that hill,
Where you think that life's gone to hell!
But eventually as time goes past,
She will help you pick yourself up, dust yourself off,
To realize these feelings will leave at last.
You will feel like a butterfly out of its cocoon
Soaring back up that great hill,
Not a moment too soon!
Yes this angel tells you, climbing back up that hill,
You will feel again!
That will be the day you start to feel sane.
Time will tell you, at it's own pace,
But you won't believe the look on your face!
The angel then sees her prayers and comforting have lifted your spirit.
From this time forward you will hold your head up.

cont.

Soon you're at the top of the hill,
Leading life at your will.
So as you go forward on life's bumpy trail,
Remember the angel will be always there.
Through all life's trials and guide your soul to prevail!

Last Poem Written — A Few Years Later

Notes

Notes

PHASE III: TO SUM IT UP!

I want to give to you a glimpse into my world since I have written these poems, a kind of what happens after.

I am writing this on 2, 20, 2020. Rereading these poems has made me feel a lot of the pain that I have written about. I still don't want it to end the way it did!

So you see, the pain is there and will never leave. Being able to stand it has gotten a lot stronger! I am taking medication for this as yet.

I am afraid to say how this will come out or what will happen next?

I believe it will go on "up" and "down" emotionally, year after year. The "highs" and "lows" are feeling as if they are farther apart. The pain is starting to level off and I do see hope on the horizon. I do believe I am going to make it. The thought of <u>leaving life</u> has totally been subdued and I know that I will see Andrea again.

Notes

Notes

PHASE IV: SUPPORTERS

A shout out to my supporters! This book of poems is the outpourings of love and loss of my daughter Andrea's sudden death by her own hand!

First and foremost my upmost thank you to my son, Erick. He has been my rock and still is. He has tried his level best to keep me on track!

I also would like to thank my brother, Ron, who has kept in touch and has been a positive enforcement for the making of this book.

I would also thank you, my Heavenly Father! You have been by my side, even when I thought you had forsaken me! My humble thanks!

It has taken a long time to compile this book because of the rereading the poems has pulled me back to the pain.

But I was so compelled to have these poems in print so hopefully it will help to see the "internal mind" of someone going through "hell" as I saw it. I share with you because hopefully you may feel that someone out there, that has gone through this type of grief, will realize they are not alone, as I did.

I pray that these insights to grief may bring peace to you as I feel they have to me.

Bless All

Notes

Notes

PHASE V: A LULLABY

A lullaby I sang to Andrea at bedtime when she was little

I have added a link so that you may hear the song that I sang to Andrea many nights as a child. Also a memory pictorial of Andrea's life.

To hear the song, scan the below QR code or go to this link: https://bit.ly/2YkoY1V

The song is *Baby Shoes* written in 1916, words by Joe Goodwin and Ed Rose, music by Al Piantadosi. Copyright MCMXVI by Shapiro, Bernstein & Co. Inc. 224 West 47th Street, New York.

"Baby Shoes"

Imagine the love of a child for its toys,
The love of a bird for its mate,
Imagine the love of a miser for gold,
Then imagine a love twice as great,
If you multiply each love a million times o'er,
It won't be half the love that a mother has for:
(to Refrain)

Refrain:
Baby shoes,
Baby shoes,
Mother will never forget them,
You have forgotten when your feet were bare,
Mother remembers, she still has a pair of
Baby shoes,
Baby shoes,
To keep them the world she'd refuse,
If she had to choose, her life she would lose,
Before she'd part with her baby's shoes.

Lone in the attic she fondles those shoes,
and wonders where her girl has gone,
And over those shoes she is saying a pray'r,
She is praying to keep her from harm,
In her heart there is gladness, tho' her eyes are wet,
Ev'ry mother remembers, while you may forget:
(to Refrain)

Goodwin, Joe; Rose, Ed; and Piantadosi, Al,
"Baby Shoes" (1916). Historic Sheet Music Collection. 132.
https://digitalcommons.conncoll.edu/sheetmusic/132

Notes

www.ingramcontent.com/pod-product-compliance
Lightning Source LLC
Chambersburg PA
CBHW051408290426
44108CB00015B/2206